DSC SPEED READS

MANAGEMENT

Interviewing

Heather Brierley

DIRECTORY OF SOCIAL CHANGE

Published by
Directory of Social Change
24 Stephenson Way
London NW1 2DP
Tel. 08450 77 77 07; Fax 020 7391 4804
email publications@dsc.org.uk
www.dsc.org.uk
from whom further copies and a full books catalogue are available.

Directory of Social Change is a Registered Charity no. 800517

First published 2011

ISBN 978 1 906294 44 1

British Library Cataloguing in Publication Data

A catalogue record for this book is available from the British Library

Cover and text designed by Kate Bass
Typeset by Marlinzo Services, Frome
Printed and bound by Martins the Printers, Berwick-upon-Tweed

All Directory of Social Change departments in London:
08450 77 77 07

Directory of Social Change Northern Office:
Research 0151 708 0136

For other titles in the DSC SPEED READ series go to:
www.dsc.org.uk/Publications/SpeedReadSeries

Contents

Introduction

Who will this book help?

This easy-to-use, practical guide will help anyone who is involved in interviewing and wants to make sure they get the right person for the right job. It takes you through an overview of the recruitment process, from what you need to do before you even start advertising the job, to what you need to do before, during and after an interview. This guide will help those who are new to selection interviewing as well as those wanting a refresher. It will be useful for those who have to select both paid staff and volunteers.

An effective selection process avoids unnecessary disruption for you and your staff caused by a mismatch between the person and the job. All too often we are under pressure to recruit staff as fast as possible. We forget to properly assess the purpose of the role and the type of person who needs to fill it. We sometimes arrive at the interview without considering the information that we need to gather from candidates, and the questions that we need to ask. This book will help those who are tight for time but want to ensure that they consider all the essentials.

What will it give you?

This book provides you with the essentials that you need to know for an effective and fair interview process. Packed with guidelines, top tips from people in the sector, real-life case studies and further resources where you can find out more, this book will ensure you recruit the right person for the job.

Chapter 1

Preparing to recruit

This chapter covers what you need to consider when reviewing jobs and the key elements needed for job descriptions and person specifications.

There are several reasons why you may be recruiting someone. There may be an area of new work that needs to be staffed. There may have been a restructure and jobs have changed. Or someone might have left your organisation and you need to replace them.

It can be tempting to recruit someone as fast as possible, but before you jump in, it is important that you plan recruitment in order to make sure that you get the right person doing the right work.

> **Top tip**
>
> **Conducting exit interviews with departing staff can provide information which helps the development of job descriptions, person specifications, the interview process and interview questions.**
>
> **Cathy Shimmin, Senior Training Consultant, DSC**

Job review

When someone leaves, it is so easy simply to assume that you need to recruit someone to exactly the same role. However, roles and organisations change. You should consider whether the purpose of the role is still relevant and whether it fits with the organisation's needs. Here are some areas for you to consider when reviewing jobs.

- Do the duties involved in the job still need to be carried out?

Case study

A museum supervisor, having never had any recruitment and selection training, had to recruit someone quickly. Not thinking about what was actually needed from the new recruit, she simply used the old job description and person specification without reviewing them. At interview, the questions asked were inappropriate and unrelated to the job description. The person selected had various performance issues and wasn't the right fit for the job.

- Are the duties appropriate to be carried out by one person? You might need more than one individual, or for the work to be divided between people who are currently employed. Perhaps this is an opportunity for a restructure.
- If the job is still needed, is it best to try to recruit internally first, or should you advertise it both internally and externally?
- Is the salary and grade of the job still appropriate?

The case study shows that it is so important to keep up-to-date with your own recruitment and selection skills, vital to make the time to review the job, and essential to ask relevant questions. Think about what you need to find out from the candidate. Ask questions that will allow candidates to provide evidence linked to the criteria set out in the job description and person specification.

Job description

The job description is a key document that you should use throughout the recruitment process. Spend time writing an accurate job description which outlines the responsibilities and requirements of the job. Speak to any staff members who work closely with whoever will hold the position, as they may have useful information about the tasks involved.

A well-written job description will help you make sure that you and the person applying for the job are clear about what they will need to do. In addition, it will be helpful in assessing the performance and training needs of the person once they are recruited.

Checklist

- ❑ Organisation name.
- ❑ Job title.

- Overall purpose of role – ideally, this should be one or two sentences to indicate the main function of the role.
- Reporting lines – there should be a section indicating the job title, department and location of who the person in the role will report to, and a section detailing any individuals, teams and departments for whom the person in the role will be responsible.
- Key responsibilities and areas of accountability – these are the duties or tasks that the person in the role will need to complete. This section forms the main bulk of the job description and is often the hardest part to write. It is helpful to have the duties listed in bullet points or numbers, with the most important tasks at the top. If the person will be responsible for more than one area, try to group the duties for each area together. Try not to list 'anything else that needs to be done' as a responsibility: this is unfair both to employer and employee.
- Performance standards – these are not essential to include, but they can be useful as they set a guideline for the quality of work you are expecting from the candidate.
- Any special conditions, for example: if travel is involved, if the person will be expected to work evenings or weekends.
- Dates and hours – you should indicate whether the job is full or part time. If the job is part time, state the number of hours (and the days, if this is not flexible) that the candidate will have to work. Start and end dates only need to be included if they are for a fixed-term contract with specific requirements.
- Salary – this can be an exact figure or a salary bracket. Not all job descriptions include the salary, but it can be useful. Candidates can then deselect themselves if the role is not within the pay bracket they are seeking.

Top tip

Get someone to read over your job description and person specification to ensure they are clear, include all the key points and are non-discriminatory.

Gemma Norgan, Assistant Manager, Natural History Museum

Top tip

There is a saying that people are 'hired for skills and fired for attitude'. Getting your person specification right and using it throughout the selection process will minimise the risk of this happening.

Maria Pemberton, Director of Operations, DSC

Top tip

Be as specific as you can with the criteria and think about how you will be able to measure whether the candidate meets them during the selection process.

Top tip

By using application forms, you are ensuring that all candidates are giving you the same information about different areas and therefore they are all starting from the same level.

Chrissie Wright, Director of Training Services, DSC

- ❑ Location.
- ❑ The date that the job description was drafted or updated.

Person specification

The person specification outlines the qualities and characteristics that the candidate needs for the job. You should include the experience, knowledge, skills, behaviours and attitudes, education and training and any other special and legal requirements necessary. It is important that you distinguish between essential and desirable criteria:

- **essential criteria** cover the areas that the applicant *must have* if they are to carry out the role to the necessary standard
- **desirable criteria** are the 'nice-to-haves' – the things that would be useful for the candidate to have, but are not vital for the role. This also helps candidates to self-select and saves time and effort on both sides.

Dos and don'ts

Do list essential criteria before desired criteria.

Do consider whether you would prefer candidates either to complete an application form or to send in a CV and covering letter.

Don't advertise the roles just anywhere – consider appropriate advertising channels to ensure that you attract the right audience.

Don't be discriminatory in your criteria – for example, don't include statements such as 'only people under 40'. Also, be aware of less obvious statements such as 'must have A levels', as this discriminates against those who have not been educated in England. You should state 'A levels or equivalent'.

Don't have a never-ending list of criteria, and group them wherever possible.

Chapter 2

Shortlisting and selecting candidates

This chapter identifies methods for shortlisting and selecting candidates and gives pointers on how to ensure a fair selection process.

Shortlisting occurs at the pre-interview stage. It involves reviewing the initial job applications and deciding who you would like to interview. Selection then follows the interview. There can be more than one round of selection: for example, if you are doing two rounds of interviews. Similar methods are used for both and so are covered together in this chapter.

When shortlisting and selecting candidates, you need to follow these steps.

1. Think about the maximum and minimum number of candidates that you want to shortlist and select at each stage. This does not need to be set in stone, but it is good to have an idea from which to work.
2. Include more than one person in the procedure. They need to be involved in, or at least be aware of and agree to, the shortlisting and selection criteria and process. They also need to have a good understanding of the requirements of the job.
3. Determine the shortlisting and selection method in advance.

Shortlisting and selection methods

Two common techniques are the Yes/No method, and the Points method.

Yes/No method

This is working through the required criteria that you have identified in the job description and person specification, and assessing whether the candidate has met them or not. You then shortlist those who meet all or most of the criteria. The downside of this method is that it gives no indication of the extent to which someone has met the criteria: for example, whether they have just about met it or well exceeded it.

Points method

This indicates how well candidates meet the criteria. It is important to have clear guidelines for what each candidate needs to demonstrate for each score. The candidates with the highest scores are then shortlisted. There are various versions of this method; here is one example where each criterion is marked out of 4.

1 = does not meet criteria
2 = partially meets criteria
3 = meets criteria
4 = exceeds criteria.

A variation on this is to use letter categories, where:

A = exceeds criteria
B = meets criteria
C = partially meets criteria
U = does not meet criteria.

Those with mainly As and Bs are shortlisted.

You also have the option of weighting the criteria, if it is more important for some criteria to be met than others. When you wrote the job description and person specification, you will have already begun to prioritise your criteria by differentiating between whether they are essential or desired.

Top tip

When shortlisting, highlight examples of exceptionally good or poor behaviours demonstrated by candidates. This helps identify any issues that need to be discussed during the final shortlist discussions. It also helps if you need to feedback to a candidate as to why they were not shortlisted.

Robert Farace, National Resourcing Manager, NHS Institute for Innovation and Improvement

In addition, you should now decide the order of importance of the criteria within those categories: for example, if you have organisational skills and good written communication skills in the essential criteria, is one of them of more, less or equal importance than the other?

When you come to scoring, you can give more weighting to those criteria which are most important. For example, if you are using the 1–4 scoring scale as outlined above and having good organisational skills is more important than the other criteria, you may want to double the score that the candidate would get against this criteria.

Top tip

Remember, when shortlisting and selecting, to look at the essential criteria first and then the desired, if needed.

Making the decision

At the end of the shortlisting or selection process you need to have assigned one of the following actions to each candidate:

- definitely interview or select
- maybe interview or select
- definitely not interview or select.

Hopefully other people shortlisting or selecting will come up with the same classification as you. If not, you will need to talk through and justify your decisions so that you can come to an agreement. With the candidates that are 'maybes', it is worth indicating whether your decision is more towards 'definitely' or 'definitely not'. If you don't have enough candidates to interview, or the person who you have selected rejects your offer, you can then look through your 'maybes'.

There may be some criteria where you are unsure of how well the candidate has met the needs of the role. Again, this is a situation where it is useful to have other people shortlisting and selecting with you, so that you can talk through what the most appropriate score may be.

Shortlisting applications takes time, especially if you have a lot of candidates. It may well be tempting to rush through applications, especially near the end of the day. Make sure that you are being fair to the candidates. Shortlist in a quiet, undisturbed location. If you have a lot of applications to go through, break up your time: for example, two hours on one day, and two hours the following day.

Where next?

For factsheets on various aspects of interviewing, see: tinyurl.com/CIPDrecruitment

Ensuring fair evaluation

There are several reasons why our evaluation of candidates can be subject to distortion. Simply being aware of the risks can help you to reduce any bias and ensure that measures are in place to evaluate candidates fairly. This bias can occur in the short-listing, interview and final selection stages; some of the typical 'traps' are shown in the following table.

Type of trap	Description of trap
'Horns and halos' effect	A candidate responds to a question either exceptionally well or exceptionally poorly and the interviewer creates a good or bad impression of the candidate. This influences how they score the rest of the candidate's answers, regardless of their quality.
Projecting yourself and/or previous jobholders	Rating people depending on whether or not they are like the interviewer or the previous jobholder. For example: 'If they went to the same university then they must be good', or 'We had someone excellent in the role and the candidate is nothing like them, so they must not be good enough'.
Logical error	Making assumptions that because someone appears to be good or bad at one thing, they also have (or do not have) skills, knowledge, experience or attitude in another area. For example, if someone demonstrates good written communication skills, they must be good at communicating verbally.

Pre-judging or going completely on first impressions	Reaching conclusions before all observations have been made: for example, the candidate demonstrates a particular behaviour once at the start of the application form or interview.
False values	A set of standards that isn't a prerequisite for the job, but which the interviewer subjectively holds regarding what the candidate should or should not be like: for example, that they will be good at the job only if they went to university.
Stereotyping or 'pigeonholing'	Categorising and grouping people who appear to be similar: for example, according to age, ethnicity or gender.
Central marking tendency	Getting into a pattern of marking candidates as average, even if they are exceptionally good or poor. This could be due to the fact that the interviewer isn't clear on the criteria, or that they are not asking enough questions to assess the candidate objectively.
Candidate contrasting	The impression of one candidate follows on to the scoring of others: for example, an interviewer may overscore an average candidate if they look at their application form or interview them after a really poor candidate, because they seem so good in comparison.
Candidate overload	Reading too many application forms or seeing too many candidates in one day. The selector is tired, frustrated and just wanting to get to the end of the process. The selector can end up being irrational or subjective in their marking of candidates.

Here are some dos and don'ts to help you avoid these traps and ensure fair evaluation of candidates throughout the selection process.

Dos and don'ts

Do remember that you are evaluating candidates against the job description, not against each other.

Where next?

Go to Businesslink for advice on many areas of recruitment and selection, including preventing discrimination and valuing diversity, shortlisting and inviting people to interview: tinyurl.com/33wfun8

Top tip

The more specific and measurable you define your selection criteria, the less scope there is for bias.

Jill Thornton, Personnel Coordinator, DSC

Do remember to keep within the guidelines of any legislation relating to discrimination.

Do ensure that you are familiar with the job description and person specification.

Do have a clear set of selection criteria and a marking scheme for how you are going to score each candidate – and stick to them.

Do make final judgements after all observations have been made.

Do treat and consider people individually.

Do remember to remove personal information from any application forms.

Don't write comments on application forms if more than one person is reviewing the applications, as this could influence them.

Don't shortlist alongside other shortlisters. Do it separately, then discuss your decisions afterwards to finalise who is through to the next stage.

Don't think that just because someone is like you, they are right for the job. Equally, don't think that because they are opposite to you, they are wrong for the job.

Don't be afraid of marking someone at either end of the scale if their performance is exceptionally good or bad.

Don't organise so many interviews in one day that by the time you reach your final candidates you are beyond caring. It puts the last candidates at an unfair advantage.

Don't make assumptions about people – base decisions on facts.

Chapter 3

Preparing to interview

This chapter covers four essential areas: involving other people in the interview process, informing the candidate, interview location and interview questions.

Involving others in the interview process

It is good to have at least two people interviewing. However, avoid leaving it until the interview itself before you talk to anyone else who is interviewing with you. Have a conversation with them prior to the interview to brief them, set expectations, make any necessary decisions and answer any queries they may have.

Make sure that everybody interviewing is aware and has relevant copies of information on the following things.

Checklist

- ❑ Your organisation's recruitment and selection policy.
- ❑ Roles and responsibilities – who is leading the interview, who is asking which questions and who is taking notes? Some organisations may have a representative from human resources (HR) who can attend the interview. It is important that everybody understands their roles in the whole process.
- ❑ The job description and person specification of the position being recruited.

Top tip

If constructing a panel interview, put yourself in the shoes of the candidate. Is the panel appropriate for the level of the job? For example, four people on a panel can be daunting.

Top tip

If trustees are involved in the interviewing, they may need extra preparation to really understand the role, as they are not part of the day-to-day running of the organisation.

Debra Allcock Tyler, Chief Executive, DSC

Top tip

Don't assume that just because someone is more senior than you, they carry out good practice in interviews. Ensure you discuss expectations for how the interview will be carried out.

Emily Kerr, Finance Projects Analyst, Cancer Research UK

- ❑ The structure of the interview.
- ❑ All of the questions being asked.
- ❑ The marking criteria and scoring sheets.
- ❑ Decision-making process after interviews.
- ❑ The process for informing successful and unsuccessful candidates (see p. 29).
- ❑ Candidates' application forms.
- ❑ Details of interview dates, times and locations.

Recording the interview

Always ensure that thorough and legible notes are taken. Agree what notes will be taken during the interview, who will take them, what level of detail is needed and how will they be taken. Some people like to have an additional person other than those interviewing to take notes: this ensures that everything is accurately recorded, and allows interviewers to concentrate fully on listening and questioning each candidate.

If you do have a separate note-taker, ensure that they are properly briefed and they have a copy of the questions. Even if you do have a separate note-taker, it can be useful to write down any key comments as you are interviewing.

First impressions

Inform key people in the building that people will be coming for interview. It is especially important that the receptionist knows who will be arriving and when. They will be the first person your candidate meets, and it is important that they make a good impression.

Inviting candidates to interview

Once you have chosen who you want to interview, you need to invite them. Give them as much notice as possible, contact them by phone, and follow up the call in writing. Ensure that you communicate all of the key information they need to know, including:

- date, time and location
- number of interviewers and their positions
- expected length of interview
- who to report to on arrival
- any preparation that the candidate needs to complete
- any relevant recruitment policies
- a map including the nearest underground or rail station information, and road directions with parking facilities.

It is good practice to notify the people who are unsuccessful in reaching the interview stage. However, you may want to wait to inform the 'maybes' until you have selected someone, because those you invite to interview might not attend and/or may not be suitable – at that point you might want to reconsider interviewing your maybes.

Top tip

As well as interviews, consider other methods for assessing the suitability of candidates: for example, numeracy or written tests, presentations or personality tests.

Interview location

Book a room that will be quiet and undisturbed, and put signs on the door when the interviews are taking place so that other people in the building will be aware that you are in session. Think about how you will set up the tables and chairs so as to put the interviewee at ease. Remember: they will already be nervous, so try to have a room set-up that is not off-putting. Also, make sure that you provide water.

Interview questions

The number of questions and wording should be defined and agreed before the interviews. You should have a set of key questions that you will ask all the candidates. In addition, you can broadly outline some possible probing questions if the need arises. These will vary, depending on the response you get from the candidate after the initial question.

Top tip

Don't try to be clever by asking obtuse questions such as: 'Should the Elgin marbles be returned to Greece?' They put candidates under unnecessary stress and have no relevance to the job.

Chrissie Wright, Director of Training Services, DSC

Effective questioning at interview is essential. It helps to ensure that you are giving candidates an equal chance to provide you with the information you need in order to assess them against the selection criteria. Remember: you are trying to give all candidates the best opportunity to demonstrate why they are the best person for the job, rather than trying to trip them up.

Use your job description, person specification and selection criteria to determine what your questions are. You should know what you are trying to find out with every question you ask. What skills, knowledge, experience and behaviours do you need your candidate to be able to demonstrate?

There are different types of interview questions that you can ask. Some are better than others – and some should be avoided at all costs.

Open questions

Open questions are those which encourage conversation and allow candidates to give some detail. They are great questions to use in interview. They often start with a Who, What, Where, Why, When or How. It is worth noting that sometimes, 'Why' questions can come across as aggressive. If possible, replace them with something like 'What are the reasons for . . . '. 'Tell me about a time . . . ' or 'Give me an example of . . . ' are also great openers.

Probing questions

Probing questions are vital. They help you check for clarity, test the validity of the response and gain further information to assess the candidate's experience accurately.

For example, you could ask two candidates an open question: 'Tell me about a time when you have organised an event.' With this question you may be trying to find out the candidate's ability to deliver an event or a piece of work on time and to the standards required, and checking for their ability to plan, manage and monitor their own and others' workloads, as well as to deal with any conflicting demands.

In this instance, one candidate may give a really full answer: they will tell you the context of the event, the ultimate results and give a detailed account of their approach and how they planned it, including how they dealt with any key stakeholders and conflicting demands.

Another candidate may give an answer that doesn't provide as much information. They will tell you the context of the event, the ultimate results and a brief overview of their approach to planning the event.

Until you ask the second candidate for more detail about their approach, to explain how they monitored other stakeholders' involvement in the project and to give an example of how they dealt with conflicting demands on their time, you have not given both candidates an equal opportunity to provide all the information about their performance, which you can then use to assess who the best candidate is.

Evidence-based questions

These are great questions to ask, they involve asking candidates to provide examples of particular situations that they have encountered, or of times when they have exhibited particular behaviours. If you pose the question properly and ask additional probing questions you can get a clear idea of how the candidate would react in, and how prepared they are for, situations relevant or common to the job.

Hypothetical questions

These involve asking a candidate to explain how they would deal with a situation, should it arise. They can

Where next?

***Successful Manager's Handbook*, B Davis, L Hellervik, J Sheard, C Skube, S Gebelein, Atlantic Books, 1996.**

***Successful Executive's Handbook*, S Gebelein, K Nelson-Neuhaus, E Sloan, Personnel Decisions International, 1999.**

Both are useful for constructing competency-based questions.

Top tip

Remember, one candidate may be more chatty and forthcoming with information, but this does not mean that they are necessarily the candidate who is best able to perform certain tasks.

give you an idea of how someone will deal with a situation, and can show their understanding of good practice. However, the answers will not be based on factual evidence; in reality, candidates will not know how they would react until actually in that situation.

Candidates will tend to give 'perfect' answers of what they think should happen rather than necessarily what they would do. If you have to use a hypothetical question, a good follow-up question is:

> *If you were to deal with the situation as you have described, what impact do you think your actions would have?*

This will help you check whether they have just given a textbook answer, or whether they have thought through their response and the impact it would create.

Top tip

Think about the order of your questions: start with some easier ones to relax the candidate and make sure the questions flow logically.

Largely, hypothetical questions are not recommended. To use hypothetical questions, you need to be a skilled interviewer, or have the support of one, to ensure the right questions are asked in order to gain useful information. Be clear about the reasons for using this type of question and the information you are expecting to obtain from candidates.

Closed questions

Closed questions are those with 'yes', 'no' or one-word answers. They do not encourage conversation, but are useful to check information. They are not likely to be a key question, but possibly a probing question.

Leading questions

Leading questions are a big 'no-no'. They do not give the candidate much of a choice in the type of response they can give, so they will simply tell you what you want to hear. For example, if you ask: 'In your role, I see you completely reviewing our approach to event management. What do you think?', the job candidate is unlikely to disagree with you.

Multiple questions

Multiple questions involve asking more than one question at time. They can confuse the candidate and lead to them missing out information. Ask one question at a time to allow the candidate to focus.

Sample questions

Here are some sample questions to help you get started. However, do not use them without considering whether they are appropriate. Do not pick questions that you like the sound of from a list that HR has given you, or simply reuse questions that you have used to recruit people into another job.

- What are your reasons for applying for this job?
- What are your greatest strengths?
- What are your weaknesses?
- How do you motivate your staff?
- How do you manage your deadlines?
- What did you learn from . . . ?
- Describe a time when you . . .
- Tell me about a time when you have had to . . .
- Give me an example of when you have had to . . .
- What is your experience in relation to . . . ?
- What is your knowledge of . . . ?

Top tip

'What are your views/ feelings/thoughts on . . . ?' is a great question to ask to check some of the criteria you are looking for in your person specification.

Cathy Shimmin, Senior Training Consultant, DSC

Top tip

Be innovative. Break out of the typical auditory process in interviews. Encourage people to show samples of their work or explain things visually on a whiteboard or flipchart.

Mark Beale, Learning and Development Consultant

Chapter 4

During the interview

This chapter covers the key skills of a successful interviewer, interview structure, dealing with 'challenging' candidates, the importance of a two-way interview and the need to treat candidates fairly.

The key skills of an interviewer

Interviewing is a skill. For some people it comes more naturally than others. You need to learn from others who are successful interviewers and practice your own technique. During the interview, there are three key skills which will help you to have a successful interview.

Where next?

DSC runs a course on interviewing skills. To find out more go to: www.dsc.org.uk/interviewing

Listening

We all listen all the time, but do we listen properly? As an interviewer you need to be actively listening to ensure that you are capturing all of the information your candidate is giving you – after all, you will need this to decide who to select for the job. You need to know what you are listening for: this will help to inform you whether you need to ask additional probing questions, if you have not heard enough information.

Ensure that there are as few distractions as possible so that you can focus on your candidate. Think about your body language: maintain eye contact without staring, look interested by leaning slightly forward and by your facial expression. Use encouraging responses such as nodding and agreeing where you can: for example, using phrases such as 'I see', 'I understand'.

Where appropriate, summarise key points to check for understanding, or ask questions which will allow you to clarify information. While it is important to take notes, try to make sure that you don't have your head in the paper all the time; finish your notes before you ask the next question so that you can listen properly to the response.

> **Top tip**
>
> **Suspend judgement on any responses you hear until the end of the interview, as this will create a barrier to listening effectively.**

Questioning

As mentioned on p. 17, it is essential that you ask the right questions during the interview. While it is important to have a planned list of questions that you will ask, you also need to be able to respond to candidates' answers by listening and then asking any further relevant questions.

> **Top tip**
>
> **Listen carefully to the questions the candidate asks you at the end of the interview. They can give you a great insight and information about the candidate.**
>
> **Chrissie Wright, Director of Training Services, DSC**

Building rapport

It is important that you build rapport with the candidate as soon as you meet them. Bear in mind that they will be nervous and that they are assessing whether your organisation is right for them too. Make sure you give your candidate a warm welcome: smile, shake their hand, greet them by name and ask them some questions which will help relax them: for example, something about their journey, weekend or interests.

Structuring the interview

It is vital to use the time that you have to interview effectively. Having some form of structure is necessary to ensure you have a focused conversation, get all the information you need to select the most appropriate

Case study

A colleague went to an interview where the interviewers told her to assume that they hadn't read her application form. They clarified that they had read it, but they wanted to ensure she had the opportunity to highlight her achievements and give examples that she had already made.

Top tip

If you are very new to interviewing, see if there is someone who can do some role-play with you to help you practise.

Mike Phillips, Associate Trainer, DSC

candidate and experience a natural flow and progression to the interview. You don't want to make your interviews icy, but the ICE structure (Introduce, Collect information, End) may help.

Introduce

- Greet and settle the candidate.
- Introduce the interviewer(s) – include their name, role in the organisation and reason for their being part of the process.
- Explain the process and the fact that you or someone else will be taking notes. Invite them to take notes if they would like.
- Give approximate timings.
- Ask the candidate if they have any questions about the process before you start.

Collect information

You need to get information from them, so:

- start with some easy questions
- use open questions and probe for more information
- listen
- concentrate on gathering evidence and examples of what they have done
- remember that the interviewer should only do 20 to 30% of the talking
- let the conversation flow.

Then they need to get information from you, so:

- give information about the job
- explain terms and conditions
- avoid jargon
- ask them what questions they have and provide the answers.

End

- Explain the next steps, when and how they will hear about the next stage.
- Confirm when and how best to contact them.
- Thank them for coming.

The three Cs: 'challenging' candidates

Sometimes you will have a challenging candidate. There are three classic challenging candidates.

The chatty candidate

It is sometimes difficult to tell whether the person is genuinely very chatty or whether they are just nervous and/or enthusiastic. Try to keep the person as focused as possible; be encouraging and polite and thank them for their answer, but move them on: for example, 'That's great; can I stop you there. Can you now tell me about . . . ?' Use phrases that will encourage them to be brief, such as: 'Can you tell me concisely about . . . ?', 'Exactly what happened in this situation . . . ?', and 'Can you summarise the results of . . . ?'

Limit the amount of information you want, for example: 'Can you give me one strength?' or 'In three sentences, tell me about . . .' Remind the interviewee gently but firmly that you only have a limited amount of time and need to get through the questions.

The clammed up candidate

Again, it is sometimes difficult to tell whether the person is genuinely very quiet or whether they are simply so nervous that they clam up. Be as encouraging as possible: smile, nod, tell them to take their time, and use positive phrases when they do provide information: for example, 'That's great' or 'Tell me more about . . .'.

Top tip

The trick with a challenging candidate is not to become frustrated and not to leave it until the end of the interview to try and manage the situation.

Top tip

Treat all candidates the same. You may be tempted to ask a candidate fewer questions if they don't seem as good as others, but everyone deserves an equal chance.

Tom Russell, HR Consultant, Russell-Sewell Limited

Top tip

Don't be afraid of silences. What probably seems like a lifetime is in reality only a few seconds. Allow people time to think of their response to your question.

If someone is really struggling to give an answer, be as reassuring as possible. If they have given an answer in their application form that they could expand on, remind them of it. It could be that they simply have gone blank and need a little prompting. Remind them where they can draw the example from, such as previous jobs, university, hobbies or volunteering. If they still aren't getting anywhere, leave the question and come back to it later.

If you are not getting as much information as you want, try another tack: ask open questions, additional probing questions or try rephrasing the question.

The cocky candidate

It can be difficult to tell whether someone is trying to be confident and has ended up going too far by being cocky, or whether they are simply being arrogant.

Top tip

Be sure to supply enough water during an interview. Nervousness can make people's mouths feel dry and make them feel uncomfortable; the act of taking a drink can calm them down and allow them time to think.

If the individual insists on saying how great they are without supplying any evidence, rephrase your questions or ask them specific questions that will encourage them to give evidence to demonstrate their capabilities. For example: 'How did you approach the task?', 'What challenges did you face, and how exactly did you overcome them?' If they are still not giving you specific information and merely telling you how wonderful they are, move on from the question. There are only so many chances you can give someone.

If their body language becomes too informal and laid back, change yours to encourage a more formal atmosphere. Should their level of cockiness spill over into inappropriate behaviour, you do not have to put up with it. You can tell them that their comments or behaviour are unsuitable for the interview, and ask them to stop.

Treating candidates equally

Remember to treat all candidates fairly. Don't discriminate and avoid bias (see p. 12).

Two-way interview: your responsibilities

What candidates see of the whole recruitment process will create an image of what your organisation is like. In a sense, the person you are interviewing is also interviewing you to see if they want to work for you and your organisation. Remember that you are representing your organisation.

Dos and don'ts

Do be well presented and observe the same behaviour as that which you would expect from a candidate – for example, switch your mobile phone off.

Do answer questions honestly. If you cannot provide an answer, find out and get back to them after the interview.

Do brief yourself and any others interviewing in order to answer obvious questions about the organisation and the terms and conditions of the job.

Do consider showing candidates around where they will be working and introduce them to a few relevant people.

Don't plan to have interviews without breaks – you need time to reflect on each candidate and allow for some over-running. If you are running late, make sure that you let the candidate know. Don't leave them waiting in reception without an explanation.

Case study

A manager of a health charity interviewed a candidate who gave very short answers to the questions. His tone and body language suggested that he didn't want to be at the interview and he wasn't interested in the job. At the end, when given the opportunity to ask the panel questions, the candidate had a long list about subjects that were only partially relevant. After the fifth question, the manager stated that this was his last one. The candidate disliked this intervention, but the manager felt candidates should earn the opportunity to ask questions: if a candidate was not prepared to cooperate with his questions, he could justifiably limit theirs, as it was his valuable time at stake.

Chapter 5

After the interview

This chapter outlines what you need to do after the interview to ensure that you select the right person for the job. It also covers how to inform both successful and unsuccessful candidates.

Keeping good records

You will probably feel quite exhausted after each interview and indeed at the end of a day of interviewing, but it is important to make sure that you have all the information recorded as soon as you have finished the interviews.

Most of your notes will have been taken during the interviews, but make sure all of them are written down in a way that ensures you have all the information recorded correctly, as they will be needed when making your final decisions on a suitable candidate. It is also important that you keep these notes, even after you have made a decision about who to offer the job to. They may be needed if someone disputes the decision you have made: for example, on grounds of discrimination. They are also useful if you need to provide any of the candidates with feedback.

Making the final decision

Once the interviews have taken place, the interview panel will need to make its final selection. How this will happen should have been decided well in advance of the interviews – certainly never after the interviews (for guidance on this part of the process, refer to p. 10 on methods of selecting candidates and ensuring fair evaluation).

Try to decide who to offer the job to as soon as possible after the interviews, as this is when the information and thoughts are fresh. Obviously, it is not a good idea to rush a decision if you are not completely sure of the best candidate, so if you do need more time, be sure to take it. If you need to hold additional interviews with candidates, arrange them.

Informing successful and unsuccessful candidates

Well done: you have finally chosen who you want to work for you. However, try not to assume that just because you have decided who you want for the job, that they are necessarily going to accept your offer.

Prior to the interview, you should have made decisions about various areas of the informing process, including the following ones.

Checklist

- ❑ Who is going to contact the interviewees, both successful and unsuccessful?
- ❑ Will offers be made subject to references or only on receipt of references?
- ❑ What probationary period will there be?
- ❑ Will offers be made subject to other conditions – for example, medical, qualification, or Criminal Records Bureau checks?

Top tip

Informing successful candidates should be a positive experience. Think how you felt when you were offered a job you really wanted. If you say you are delighted to offer them the role, make sure you sound delighted!

Tom Russell, HR Consultant, Russell-Sewell Ltd

Where next?

HR for non-HR Specialists, DSC training course: www.dsc.org.uk/nonhrspecialists

Top tip

Make time to give feedback. Just ensure you deliver it effectively. Think before opening your mouth! Remember: giving feedback reflects well on your organisation. Candidates value information that helps them improve.

Sophie Bradwell, Campaigning Manager, Cancer Research UK

Where next?

For information on many areas of selection including sample rejection letters and feedback, see: www.businessballs.com/interviews.htm

- ❑ How much information will be offered to unsuccessful interviewees in terms of feedback? Who will give this feedback?

Key steps to informing candidates

It is best to contact the successful candidate by phone. Be clear about the conditions of the offer: for example, if it is subject to references. Some candidates will accept the offer immediately, but others may want to think it over. Let them know when you need a decision by, and if there are any areas that you cannot negotiate on: for example, salary.

Confirm the offer in writing, along with any other relevant details such as terms and conditions. Also, ask for their acceptance in writing. Then, carry out any essential checks such as references, qualifications and security.

It is worth waiting until you have a final confirmation from your first choice before rejecting all of the other candidates, but don't leave them hanging for too long. Contact the reserve candidates to let them know when you will give them your final decision, and again when you have your final decision.

Contact any candidates who you are definitely not going to employ, even if your first choice turns you down. This can be done in writing.

Thank all the candidates for their time: it is good practice to offer to give them feedback, and to ensure that it is specific, accurate and concise. Do bear in mind that we are only human and can only take so much criticism – if you are rejecting a candidate, try to let them know how they impressed you, as well as being clear on the reasons for rejection, and what they need to work on in the future.

Chapter 6

Selecting volunteers

This chapter outlines some key considerations for those selecting volunteers.

Key considerations

Surely you don't need to worry about selecting volunteers? You just accept anyone who is willing to help? Right? Wrong. While we are extremely grateful for the valuable work that our volunteers do, we have to be realistic. Not everyone will be suitable for particular roles. Volunteers need to be managed, just the same as staff: this takes time, energy, effort and resources.

Imagine this scenario: 20 people want to volunteer with you, but you only have work for 10 people. Because they are volunteers, you feel you should recruit all of them. Unfortunately, you are likely to end up with 20 bored, unhappy and ineffective volunteers because you have tried to spread the work too thinly and they were expecting to be involved and active. You then have to spend extra time managing them, taking you away from other tasks that you need to complete.

It is far better to select 10 of the most effective volunteers so that the work is done to the highest possible standards, they are engaged, and you aren't spending unnecessary extra time managing them.

Where next?

***Recruiting Volunteers*, F Dyer, U Jost, DSC, 2006.**

Managing Volunteers, DSC training course: www.dsc.org.uk/managingvolunteers

Volunteering England website: tinyurl.com/34ldyfp

Top tip

If volunteers do not live up to expectations at interviews, review your recruitment process to ensure you are sending the right message about what the role is about.

Moyra Weston, Associate Trainer, DSC

Top tip

Ask 'What do you hope to gain from the experience?', 'What would you like to do?' and 'What can you offer?' to clarify volunteers' motivations and manage expectations.

Terry Gilfoyle, Learner Development Coordinator, Smart CJS

Do remember that in many cases, if you do not select your volunteers carefully, it can end up being detrimental to your organisation and inhibit you from achieving your vision. You don't necessarily need to have formal interviews, but you still need to ask the right questions and have the same high selection standards as paid staff.

Dos and don'ts

Do plan your volunteer recruitment instead of just jumping in.

Do be clear on the role that your volunteers will fill and the methods you will use to select volunteers.

Do make sure that you encourage volunteers to keep in touch with your organisation if you feel they might be suitable to work with you at another time – tell them to try again in the future, or ask if they would like to be on a waiting list in case other opportunities should come up.

Don't refer to 'job descriptions' but 'role profiles' – for legal reasons, it is important to be careful about the language that you use. Volunteers are not employees, and do not have jobs or contracts.

Don't forget that volunteers are not subject to employment legislation. However, you still need to treat them fairly. You also need to make sure that you are not offering anything or using practices which could be mistaken for treating them as an employee.

Don't feel you need to take on every volunteer. Inform everyone of whether they have been successful or not in volunteering with you. If they may be suitable for another role, discuss this as an option.